creat!ve  confirmation

Youth Journal

My Confirmation Journey

by _____

Augsburg Fortress, Minneapolis

Contents

**Creative Confirmation Series
Youth Journal**

Editors: Mary Nasby Lohre and Julie A. Lindesmith
Designer: Connie Helgeson-Moen
Cover photographers: © Robb Helfrick (front); ©
CLEO Freelance Photo (back)

Scripture acknowledgment: Unless otherwise
marked, scripture quotations are from New
Revised Standard Version Bible, copyright 1989
Division of Christian Education of the National

Council of the Churches of Christ in the United
States of America. Used by permission.

Introduction

Welcome to confirmation. Welcome to an important tradition within the Lutheran church. Welcome to a journey of faith that includes new questions, discoveries, relationships, responsibilities, and possibilities.

This *Youth Journal* is one of your companions on your confirmation journey. In the section at the back, keep track of what you study, your classmates, and the events and memories that are important to you during confirmation. The remaining pages will guide you in keeping a record of the questions, thoughts, and discoveries you have about the topics you study.

This journal may be the beginning of a lifelong practice for you. Many Christians write in a journal on a regular basis. Why?

◆ Writing in a journal can help you focus your thoughts on the important things you have read and discussed with others. Sometimes, writing helps you clarify what you think and believe.

◆ A journal is a place to record those questions that stay with you after the class discussion ends.

◆ A journal is a safe place to put your feelings into words. Reading back over your journal may help you gain a new insight on a troubling or challenging topic.

◆ A journal can also become a reminder of your need to pray.

Writing in a journal may be new for you, but don't worry. Enjoy it as part of your confirmation journey. Remember, the point of confirmation is not to determine who knows the most, or who is worthy to belong to the church. Your confirmation journey is your time to grow in the faith God gave you in baptism. Use this journal to help you make the most of this journey.

Focus on this Genesis 2:18-25 (Creation)

Imagine this It is important for homes to be loving, nurturing places for children as well as husbands and wives. Think about your family and answer these questions:

◆ How do you and the other members of your family express love for one another?
◆ What could you do to make your home a more loving and nurturing place?

Focus on this Genesis 32:9-32 (Jacob wrestles with God)

Imagine this Think of one struggle you have had with someone in your family. Examine three important relationships in that struggle: the one you have with yourself, the one you have with the family member, and the one you have with God.

◆ First, ask yourself how *you* view each relationship. Then, ask how *God* might view each relationship.
◆ Where are these two perspectives the same? Where are they different? What does this tell you about God's will for your life?

Focus on this Genesis 37:1-28 (Joseph and his brothers)

Imagine this Many young people know very little about the experiences of their parents, grandparents, or guardians when they were young. Ask these questions of your parent, grandparent, or another trusted adult:

◆ What was her or his family life like when she or he was your age?
◆ How is your daily life different than or similar to hers or his?

Focus on this Genesis 39 (Potiphar's wife)

Imagine this
People in the Scriptures had all the same feelings and ambitions as people today. God often works behind the scenes directing the dramas of our lives in ways we can't always see or appreciate at the time. Ask your parent or another trusted adult:

◆ Were you ever saved in a really tough situation through some totally unexpected turn of events?
◆ How did you handle temptations when you were my age?

Focus on this Genesis 41:1-45 (Pharaoh's dreams)

Imagine this God worked through the events of Joseph's life and the lives of the people around Joseph. Ask your parent or another trusted adult:

◆ How did you decide what to do when you finished high school?
◆ Where did those decisions end up taking you?

Focus on this Genesis 45:1-15 (Family reconciliation)

Imagine this The desire to be connected to others and to have harmony restored is often stronger than the desire to get even. Ask a parent or trusted adult:

◆ How did your family resolve disagreements when you were growing up?
◆ How do you decide what to do about disagreements in the family now?

Focus on this Genesis 45:16—46:7 (Israel in Egypt)

Imagine this Change is part of everyone's life. Some changes cause pain and discomfort, but changes can help make our lives better as we learn to accept them. Ask your parent or trusted adult:

◆ What big changes happened in your family when you were growing up?
◆ How did that affect you and your family, and how does it affect the family you live in now?

Focus on this 1 Samuel 1:1-20 (Hannah's child)

Imagine this Hannah was faithful to God by trusting God to help her and her unborn child. Sometimes what we think God is asking of us isn't what God has in mind at all. God wants us to trust God with our lives. Ask your parent or another trusted adult:

◆ When you were my age, what did you want to become as an adult?
◆ If you were to get all the money and time you needed, what would you like to do now?

Focus on this 1 Samuel 3:1-18 (Samuel's call)

Imagine this God calls each of us to some special purpose. Sometimes God calls through other people who see things in us that we aren't aware of ourselves. God also uses us to do this for others. Ask your parent or another trusted adult:

◆ Did you ever have a really strong conviction that you should do something?
◆ Who helped you figure out some things you were good at doing when you were my age?

Focus on this 2 Samuel 11:2-21 (David and Bathsheba)

Imagine this It has been said that all that is necessary for evil to flourish is for good people to do nothing. It's easy for us to see ourselves as victims, but it's harder to see ways in which we may be victimizing others. Sometimes we do this by failing to act when we could have prevented trouble. Ask your parent or another adult:

◆ Did you ever get in trouble when you were my age because you didn't try to stop someone from something harmful they were doing?

◆ Did you ever get in trouble because your friends didn't talk you out of doing something wrong?

Focus on this 2 Samuel 12:1-15 (Nathan and the king)

Imagine this We all get caught up with our own wants. The crucial moment comes when we are confronted about our actions and attitudes. Do we deny our wrongdoing, or do we confess and ask for forgiveness? David was a great leader because he confessed and asked for forgiveness. Ask a parent or another adult:

◆ What was one of the hardest things you ever had to do when you were my age?
◆ If you could change any unjust situation today, what would you change?

Focus on this 1 Kings 3:3-14 (Solomon's prayer)

Imagine this The world teaches that success comes from having more possessions and being more powerful than others. This leads to divisions among people. God teaches that rulers must lead with wisdom, compassion, and concern for everyone. Ask your parent or another adult:

◆ What adults influenced you most when you were my age?
◆ What can you remember about that person's wisdom, compassion, and concern for others?

Focus on this Exodus 3:1-17 (The call of Moses)

Imagine this As Christians, we are all called to set people free. Moses had a burning bush to tell him what he was to do. Sometimes, we may overlook signs from God that are just as obvious.

◆ How do you find out when people close to you are oppressed by fear, loneliness, or physical need? Do you recognize any of those signs of oppression in yourself?
◆ What resources do you have available to you that could lead others (as well as yourself) to freedom?

Focus on this Exodus 7:8—11:10 (The plagues in Egypt)

Imagine this Exodus tells of a God who acts through nature to set people free. Most of us are more like the stubborn and power-hungry Pharaoh than we care to admit.

◆ What natural plagues threaten your world?
◆ How could these plagues be a sign of the ultimate power of God over the natural world, the world community, and the emotional, spiritual, and physical boundaries of your experiences?

Focus on this Exodus 14:10-29 (Deliverance at the sea)

Imagine this When we read about God rescuing the Israelites from the raging sea and Pharaoh's soldiers, the story may seem like a fairy tale to us. Our own narrow escapes from catastrophe never seem quite so dramatic; or do they?

◆ When was the last time you or someone close to you had to face possible hardship, illness, or failure before being saved?
◆ How does your baptism affect the way you respond to situations that test your faith in God's ability or willingness to provide for all your needs?

Focus on this Judges 4:1-22 (Deborah)

Imagine this God defeats some mighty forces in order to free people. The Old Testament records these defeats, including the violence that was a part of those victories. How do we reconcile that brutality with the destructive violence in our world that we see recorded daily by the media?

◆ What does the violence in our times have to do with the violence that erupted in the Garden of Eden (between Cain and Abel) and at Jesus' crucifixion?
◆ Does the violence in the Old Testament stories suggest that violence is part of God's plan for our lives?

Focus on this 1 Samuel 17:1-49 (David and Goliath)

Imagine this
Israel was to trust in God's strength during difficult times, but only David, the young shepherd, took God's promised presence seriously.

◆ Who reminds you of God's dependability when things look bleak for you or people you love?

◆ What "giant" lurks in the shadows of your life? Write a prayer that asks God to help you identify sources of help, then find and accept help from the people or experiences that will help you face and conquer that giant with the strength of God's presence and power.

Focus on this Psalm 23 (The good shepherd)

Imagine this Jesus calls himself the good shepherd. He
wants to be part of our lives, lead us in the right direction, comfort
us when we are troubled, and help us face our lives with hope and
courage.

◆ Who or what shepherds you? Is it someone in your family, the
   expectations of your friends, or the call of the media?
◆ What would make you feel more in touch with Jesus' direction,
   comfort, and help?

Focus on this 2 Kings 5:1-19 (Elisha and Naaman)

Imagine this
This Bible story reminds us that at different times in our lives we may require different kinds of healing: healing for our bodies, minds, and spirits.

◆ What kind of healing have you experienced most recently? What kind of healing do you need now?
◆ What might you do in your life today to bring God's healing to your friends, family, or world?

Focus on this
Daniel 3:1-30 (Three young men in the fiery furnace)

Imagine this
This Bible story describes a time when Jewish people were persecuted for worshiping God alone and not the pretender gods of the Persian ruler. The young men's faithfulness caused them to be tested with the threat of a fiery death. God intervened and saved them.

◆ When has your faith been under fire? What kind of prayers did you offer or think of during those times?
◆ Were you able to see God at work strengthening and protecting you? Can you see that now?

Focus on this Mark 5:1-20 (Jesus heals)

Imagine this
As Christians, we believe that Christ has the power to free us from the evils that keep us from being what God intended for us to be. Those evils control us by consuming our energy, our time, and our resources.

◆ What evil obsession has you wrapped around its finger?
◆ How does knowing that you are created in the image of God compare with the way you feel about yourself when the obsession is in control of your mind and heart?

Focus on this John 11:1-53 (Jesus raises Lazarus)

Imagine this Martin Luther said that as we wake up each morning, we should make the sign of the cross to remember the waters of baptism that have made us new people again, made alive to live a great life.

◆ How many mornings in the last week did you wake up feeling like a new person?
◆ What kind of experiences, attitudes, and opportunities remind you that you are a loved and forgiven child of God who has new life now and forever?

Focus on this Mark 15:1-41 (Jesus' death)

Imagine this In Jesus' time, the cross was an instrument of punishment and death. Yet, God surprises us by using it to bring eternal life to all people.

◆ What other surprising things does the story of Jesus' death bring to your mind?
◆ If you live a Christ-like life, what surprising responses can you give when you experience disappointment, anger, fear, or frustration?

Focus on this Matthew 28:1-10 (The empty tomb)

Imagine this The women who came to the empty tomb were shocked at what they found. They were overcome with feelings of fear and joy. When we discover the truth, it can be a shocking experience.

◆ On your confirmation journey, you will come face to face with the truth about God and your relationship to God. What one idea has seemed shocking to you?

◆ The women at the tomb quickly shared the truth they discovered. What will you do with the truth you have found?

Focus on this Romans 8 (Free at last)

Imagine this The early Christians lived with hope even though their lives were filled with danger and difficulties because of their belief in Jesus.

◆ Do you live confidently, even though problems and pressures are a part of your life?

◆ How does your hope of eternal life affect the way you face each day?

Focus on this Deuteronomy 8 (Remembering God's gifts)

Imagine this You are at the beginning of life. The future holds many promises as well as some risks!

◆ What are some of the promises and risks that you will face in the years ahead?
◆ What gifts of God make it possible for you to have hope in the future, even though you know that it is part of human nature to be sinful?

Focus on this Isaiah 2:1-4 (Swords into plowshares)

Imagine this People who think they have to depend on themselves for all things build tools of destruction. People who trust in God to meet their needs transform tools of destruction into instruments of peace.

◆ What issues are the swords of destruction in your family, group of friends, and community?

◆ What can you do to encourage peacemaking rather than conflict in each of these situations?

Focus on this Amos 5:14-24 (Justice)

Imagine this
Amos taught people to avoid idolatry and work for justice in the world. But in all times (and now), people are tempted to trust themselves more than God to meet their needs.

◆ When was the last time you watched someone (maybe even yourself) take advantage of someone else to get what he or she wanted?
◆ What gifts of God make it possible for you to have hope in the future, even though you know that it is part of human nature to be sinful?

Focus on this Matthew 5:1-12 (The Beatitudes)

Imagine this We are blessed by God. That means that God has equipped us to make a difference in this world. We are equipped with the hope that God brings to us in forgiveness and the promise of new life. That helps us see everything in a new way.

◆ How does being a Christian change the way you look at all the struggles and suffering that are a part of life?
◆ How can you, a blessed child of God, be a blessing to others?

Focus on this Matthew 10 (Sent out)

Imagine this This Bible story reminds us that we are called by God to be a *witness* to the gospel, not a judge. Witnesses tell others what they have experienced and what they believe to be true.

◆ Who is the best Christian witness that you know? What makes that person a good witness?
◆ What do other people know about your beliefs in God from your actions, words, and attitudes?

Focus on this Matthew 28:16-20 (The Great Commission)

Imagine this When we have a huge task to accomplish, it helps if we can depend on someone to be there to encourage, guide, and support our efforts while we work. In this passage, Jesus promises to be with us as we bring the message of God's love to all people.

◆ Who in your life gives you the encouragement and support you need to help you witness to your faith in Jesus?
◆ What part does prayer play in your daily life?

Focus on this Luke 24:36-52 (Jesus appears to his disciples)

Imagine this We can open the minds of others to see Jesus by demonstrating repentance and forgiveness in his name.

◆ Who shows you how to be sorry about having hurt others, and who shows you how to be forgiving?
◆ What opportunities do you have to show someone else how repentance and forgiveness work?

Focus on this Acts 9:1-31 (The conversion of Saul)

Imagine this Conversion turns us around to take a new path on life's journey. Sometimes, that is what it takes to get our attention away from "the way we have always done things."

◆ What takes up most of your time and energy?
◆ Would you be willing to change the routine of your life without first having a drastic change interrupt the normal pattern of your activities?

Focus on this Galatians 3:23-29 (The law's purpose)

Imagine this We are all equal in Christ. We are defined by Christ, not the law. That gives us the freedom to meet one another on equal ground.

◆ Why is it threatening for some people to find themselves in a community where all people are equal?
◆ What is it that unifies and equalizes all who follow Jesus?

Focus on this Hebrews 11:1-16; 12:1-2 (A cloud of witnesses)

Imagine this Like an Olympic athlete finishing a race before a crowd of people from all countries and centuries, we run the path Jesus prepared. For Jesus, who accepted the cross on our behalf, waits at the finish line to welcome us home.

◆ Identify active members of your congregation who fit the following categories: one person who is no longer living, one who is over 70, one who is between 35 and 45, one who is between 20 and 30, and one who is your age.

◆ Find out who coached them along their faith journeys. What qualities made those people good faith coaches? How many of those qualities do you share with others on their faith journeys?

Focus on this Revelation 21:1-5 (A new heaven and a new earth)

Imagine this This passage says that all of creation will be totally reunited with God. This new heaven and earth are described like the camera's scanning at the start of a movie. Landscapes make way for more detailed pictures, focusing on God dwelling intimately among God's people.

◆ If you were filming the opening scenes of this movie, what scenes would you choose for the opening shots? What landscapes would highlight the creation in desperate need of God's re-creation, and what individuals could highlight people who would welcome God's promised new life?
◆ Brainstorm an outline for the script of this imagined movie. Would you tell the story with a documentary, a short story, or a filmed ballet or modern dance?

Focus on this The Second Commandment and its explanation

Imagine this When we keep God's name precious to us, we are not tempted to forget that God is precious to us and that God's power is given to us.

◆ When you hear someone swear or use God's name in vain, do you think of that person respecting God's power or trying to seem more powerful than God?
◆ If you recognize and appreciate God's power that has been made ours by the life, death, and resurrection of Jesus Christ, what kind of things are possible for you to accomplish when you are with your family and your friends?

Focus on this The Fifth Commandment and its explanation

Imagine this God cares so much for all of the creation that he devoted a whole commandment to forbidding any behavior that kills or harms any part of the created world.

◆ How did God provide for renewal in the natural world and the relationships between individuals and God, as well as between individuals?
◆ Write or draw something that identifies your role in the re-creation or renewal of an abused or damaged part of the creation or a relationship you have.

Focus on this The Seventh Commandment and its explanation

Imagine this When we treat others with fairness and justice, we give them a chance to contribute to the well-being of everyone.

◆ Browse through a recent copy of your community's newspaper. Look for articles, cartoons, or ads that refer to fairness or justice. Are there more that highlight fairness and justice, or more that highlight unfairness and injustice?
◆ Brainstorm a list of your activities in the last week. How many opportunities have you given other people to contribute to the good of your family or community?

Focus on this The Apostles' Creed

Imagine this It is important to know what we believe about God, especially as we encounter beliefs that are different from ours. The Apostles' Creed tells us about the one God who reveals himself as Father, Son, and Holy Spirit.

◆ How many new religious movements or cults are active in your community? Do you know what beliefs those groups have? Could you describe your beliefs to them?
◆ What would you say if someone asked you, "How would you describe your God?"

Focus on this The First Article of the Apostles' Creed and its explanation

Imagine this Most of us like to have our own stuff—things that we control. Yet, the Creed indicates that everything in the creation belongs to God, who gives us what we need. Therefore, we are caretakers, not owners, of all that we have.

◆ What do you own?
◆ What kind of a caretaker are you?

Focus on this The Second Article of the Apostles' Creed and its explanation

Imagine this On the cross Jesus takes our sin upon himself and gives us his righteousness, innocence, and peace. That's quite an exchange policy!

◆ Remember a time when you had to exchange something. Describe your feelings before, during, and after that experience.
◆ Think of Jesus' life, death, and resurrection as an exchange experience. Describe your feelings about that experience.

Focus on this The Second Petition of the Lord's Prayer and its explanation

Imagine this The public outpouring of the Holy Spirit upon the early followers of Jesus on Pentecost during and following the earthly life of Jesus made it possible for the people to be delivered from the lasting power of evil. Baptism brings us the same blessing.

◆ What do you know about your baptism? Have you stayed close to your sponsors?

◆ Write to or talk to your sponsors or someone else who was present at your baptism. Learn from them how your life was transformed by baptism.

Focus on this The Fourth Petition of the Lord's Prayer and its explanation

Imagine this This petition urges us to adopt the attitude of "thanks-living."

◆ What do you think that attitude looks like to people who observe it in others? Find some examples in the news of people who live like that.
◆ How would the people around you be affected if you lived with a more thankful attitude? How would life be different for you?

Focus on this The Sixth Petition of the Lord's Prayer and its explanation

Imagine this Martin Luther says that the devil, the world, and our flesh try to deceive us and draw us away from firm faith in God. That is why we need to ask God to help us when such times of testing occur.

◆ How does the power of evil approach you? Where do you feel most vulnerable or likely to be swept away into attitudes or behaviors that are not healthy?

◆ How do you prepare for tests? How can you adapt those behaviors to prepare you to wrestle with the power of evil?

Focus on this The Sacrament of Baptism

Imagine this Baptism is also our welcome into the church—the community of all persons who have been so rescued.

◆ Find out as much as you can about the people in your congregation. Research the members' cultural or racial backgrounds, family size, vocations, hobbies, gifts, and volunteer activities.
◆ If you were going to plan a get-acquainted event to help members learn about and enjoy one another, what kind of activities and follow-up efforts would you schedule? How could this event help your church family grow?

Focus on this The Sacrament of Holy Communion

Imagine this Holy Communion is the original health food. When we go to the Supper, we are refreshed through the healing power of this gift of life.

◆ Draw a mental picture of the last time your congregation shared the Lord's Supper. Beginning with the words of institution, make a list of all the things that people did during that part of the service. Why do you think it is important to do those things?
◆ How does this spiritual health food nourish the lives of believers after the meal is over? What does it give us strength to do or be?

Focus on this Office of the Keys

Imagine this Jesus gave to the whole church (and that includes us) one of the keys to life: the gift of being able to forgive one another.

◆ How many keys do you have? Assign each of those keys a problem relationship in your life.
◆ How could forgiveness help you unlock an unhealthy relationship in your family or group of friends?

Focus on this Using your senses

Imagine this
You have five senses: sight, smell, hearing, taste, and touch. Lutheran worship uses all of them. *(Sight: reading the words of the hymns; hearing: listening to the gospel; touch: sharing the peace; taste: eating bread and wine during Holy Communion; smell: burning incense or candles.)*

◆ What difference would it make to the worship service if one of those elements was eliminated from the experience?
◆ Which element do you appreciate most, and how might you make worship more meaningful in your congregation?

Focus on this Blueprint for worship

Imagine this As we worship, we experience many truths about the life of faith: it is a celebration, it is painful, and we need God and others. The mood and the message of the liturgy helps us understand that liturgical worship offers rhythm for our lives of faith.

◆ What is painful about a life of faith? Why do we need God and others?
◆ How do you celebrate your faith?

Focus on this Scriptures alive

Imagine this Each Sunday we listen to God's Word for us in Old Testament, Psalms, New Testament, and Gospel readings. Varying the ways that scripture readings are presented can help communicate the gospel more clearly.

◆ What scripture passage do you remember best? How was it presented to you?
◆ What would you be willing to do to help the Scriptures come alive for others in your congregation?

Focus on this Advent

Imagine this Advent is celebrated the four weeks before Christmas. It is the beginning of the church year, and it is a season of preparation and anticipation. The liturgical color for Advent is royal blue or purple, reminding us that we are awaiting the coming of royalty into our midst. During this time, we remember God's promise to send a savior and the way God fulfilled that promise.

◆ Do you benefit more from anticipating an event or experiencing it? Give an example.
◆ Why do doctors make sure patients are prepared for surgery, and how will that preparation affect the outcome of the procedure? What does this example have to do with God's promise?

Focus on this Epiphany

Imagine this
Symbolized by a star, Epiphany is a time when we travel with the Wise Men to see a most amazing wonder: God in human form, living in the midst of creation. Epiphany becomes our telescope to search for that which is far off, and yet right in front of us.

◆ Think of the last time you lost something and had to search for it. What strategy did you use for your search?

◆ Many people retrace their steps when they are looking for something. As Christians, we follow Jesus' steps, or teachings, as we look for God's presence in our lives. How could Epiphany be a more meaningful time in your life?

Focus on this The Sacrament of Holy Communion

Imagine this Communion provides for us a way to remember the sacrificial lifestyle led by Jesus the Christ. It is a practice shared within Christian faith communities that unites Christians around the world.

◆ What did you think about Communion when you were a young child? How have your feelings about the experience changed?
◆ How many of your activities link you to other members of God's family who live far away? What benefit is there in doing something together with those Christians?

Focus on this Confession and forgiveness

Imagine this Confession and forgiveness are two sides of the same coin. Without confession there is no forgiveness; but without forgiveness, confession is worthless. Forgiveness is a difficult task for all people, but God's forgiveness of us gives us reason to be forgiving with one another. The ritual of confession and forgiveness in Lutheran worship reminds us to be forgiving people.

◆ When we confess, God forgives. When was the last time you confessed to something, and what kind of response did you get?
◆ How many rituals do you practice in your daily activities? Why do you do those things? What effect do those activities have on your attitude and choices?

Focus on this Kyrie liturgy

Imagine this

The kyrie is a cry to God to listen to our prayers and a way to focus our worship and praise on issues of our community. Listening is a key skill for the kyrie. A congregation that worships using the kyrie believes that God is listening to these prayers.

◆ How well do you and your congregation listen to the prayers and cries of people around you?
◆ Look at the kyrie that your congregation uses in worship. Write your own kyrie. Offer it to your pastor for use by your congregation.

Focus on this Listening and telling

Imagine this Story sticks and sacred pipes are used in Native American story-telling cultures as a way to hold attention and respect. Whoever holds the object is the storyteller, and everyone listens to what it is that that person has to say.

◆ Which objects have meaning in your household? What encourages your family members to listen when a story is being told?

◆ What kinds of stories receive the most attention in your home? What faith story do you have to tell?

Focus on this Journal writing

Imagine this Keeping a journal helps people remember
and share the stories of their lives.

◆ How does writing a story help you notice details that you might
   have missed when you created or experienced it?
◆ How does it feel to share a written story with someone else?
   Does a story change when it is shared?

Focus on this John 3:1-17 (Nicodemus visits Jesus)

Imagine this Some people expect worship to provide them with all the answers they need for life. Nicodemus knew, however, that part of worship is to ask questions. It is also being ready to let God speak the answers to us.

◆ Look at a recent church bulletin. How many parts of the service allow followers of Jesus to ask questions about the life of faith?

◆ What questions would you like to ask Jesus?

Focus on this Isaiah 64:1-9 (A prayer of penitence [sorrow] for sins)

Imagine this Christians pray at mealtime, bedtime, worship, times of joy, sadness, illness, uncertainty, thanksgiving, and so forth.

◆ When do you pray? What kind of pose do you choose for your prayers?
◆ If God is the potter, what kind of attitudes and poses might be most helpful if we want God to sculpt something useful and beautiful out of our lives?

Focus on this Gospel joy

Imagine this The stories of Jesus' life, death, and resurrection have brought ripples of joy to the lives of people throughout the generations.

◆ Think of a particular happy experience you would like to share with God.
◆ Write a circle prayer about that joy—a prayer that begins in the center of the page and moves outward from that center.

Focus on this Self-expression

Imagine this The Psalms are full of many of the same
ideas and feelings that we experience today. In their worship, the
people of God expressed those personal feelings and beliefs.

◆ Write a psalm for today that shares your feelings and beliefs.
◆ Why would your personal psalm be a good resource for your
  personal devotions?

Focus on this Genesis 11:1-9 (The Tower of Babel)

Imagine this The origin of the variety of languages in the world is in part a mystery. Genesis 11 tells us when people became prideful and thought that by building a tower to the heavens they could become godlike, God caused the people to begin to speak in different languages. In this way, God reminded the people who was still in charge.

◆ What words do you use to separate yourself from your parents, your siblings, strangers, and maybe even God?
◆ What kinds of verbal and nonverbal communication will help you build better relationships with others—including God?

Focus on this Media influences

Imagine this Language used in media and music can both build community and create a sense of inadequacy.

◆ Where do you get the most positive messages about yourself? Do any of those messages come from the media?
◆ The media reflect the values of the culture. What values of youth culture are reflected in the words and images the media present to you? How does that compare with the words and images your faith community uses when they describe you?

Focus on this Memory tricks

Imagine this Humor and nonsense are excellent tools for helping us remember the things we need to know. For example, if we don't know the order of the petitions of the Lord's Prayer or the Ten Commandments, we won't understand how these parts of the catechism fit together. We may not be able to appreciate how the Commandments move in ever-widening circles, from a concern about our nearest neighbors (our God and our family) to concern about neighbors that are farther away.

◆ Think of a childhood rhyme, song, or puzzle that helped you remember some important kind of information when you were younger.
◆ Create a memory trick using one of these techniques to help you remember the topics included in an important part of your faith story, such as the Apostles' Creed, the Ten Commandments, or the Lord's Prayer.

Focus on this Telling God's story

Imagine this
Throughout the ages, many of God's people have been unable to read. Therefore, Scripture has always needed to be shared by oral reading. The poetry of the Bible is not based on rhyme and mechanical rhythm, but on a balance of ideas. Parallel ideas, some complementary and some contradictory, are put side by side so as to form a logical rhythm. These ideas are more memorable when they are read aloud and heard.

◆ Upon what skills do we depend when we listen to (rather than read) Scripture?
◆ What scripture texts stand out in your memory as being surprising or more interesting to hear?

Focus on this Job 38—41 (God answers Job)

Imagine this

Everything was taken away from Job, a blameless and upright man who feared God and avoided evil (Job 1—37). Though friends faulted him, Job firmly held to his claim of innocence and refused to give up on God. When God finally answered Job's cry for conversation, God rehearsed for Job what God had done as creator of the universe. Only then did Job begin to understand the power and faithfulness of God in his misfortune.

◆ What experiences, observations, and people tempt you to question God's faithfulness? Can you see God's power and faithfulness in that misfortune?

◆ Who reminds you of Job by believing in God's promise of blessing even when everything seems to deny it?

Focus on this Judges 5 (The song of Deborah)

Imagine this Deborah was one of the leaders in early Israelite history who were called judges. Her activity is recorded in Judges 4–5. She and Barak, the army commander, led Israel to victory over its enemies, the Canaanites. Deborah rallied the forces of Israel that made the land safe. Then, together with Barak, she sang a hymn composed to celebrate the Lord's victory for the people (Judges 5).

◆ What daily battles do you fight?

◆ God gave Deborah the faith to inspire others to victory. How does the faith God gives you affect your daily life?

Focus on this Jonah 4 (Jonah's anger and God's response)

Imagine this The Lord told Jonah to go to Nineveh to cry out against the wickedness of the people. Nineveh was to the east, but Jonah took off to the west! Jonah finally went to Nineveh and declared its impending destruction. When the people repented, God did not destroy the city. Jonah got angry. Then God helped Jonah realize that the people of Nineveh (whose repentance the Lord wanted and rewarded) were more important than the comforts Jonah sought.

◆ God actively participated in the lives of Nineveh's people by sending Jonah to warn them and then allowing them to survive. What problem did Jonah and Nineveh's people share?

◆ Think of jealousy as a two-way mirror. Then think of someone who makes you feel jealous. What does that jealousy tell you about that other person? What does that jealousy tell you about yourself?

Focus on this Matthew 15:21-28 (A woman's faith)

Imagine this A woman who had a sick daughter came to see Jesus. The disciples wanted Jesus to send the woman away, but she persisted and finally was able to speak with Jesus. Jesus acknowledged the woman's great faith and granted her request for her daughter's healing.

◆ Faith gives people courage. What actions sprang from this woman's courage?
◆ Who is the most courageous person you know? Do you think that faith inspires that person's courage? Does your faith inspire courage in you?

Focus on this Scripture, authority, and testament

Imagine this When we use the term *scripture*, we refer to sacred or religious writings. *Authority* is a source of knowledge or a power or influence over someone. *Testament* means covenant or agreement. The Old Testament includes stories describing the old agreement between God and the people. The New Testament includes stories describing the new agreement with God, one that centers on our savior Jesus Christ.

◆ What authority does Scripture have in your life?
◆ How is your life story a testament to your agreement with God?

Focus on this Sin and salvation

Imagine this

Sin is more than just breaking a law. Sin is separation from God. In this separation, we are also separated from neighbor, self, and the world. Sin is a deed as well as a condition. Salvation is the answer to sin. Salvation is the bridge that fills the gap between humankind and God. The bridge was built by God through the life, death, and resurrection of Jesus Christ.

◆ What words, actions, and emotions come to mind when you think about sin?
◆ What bridges does salvation build between you and the important people in your life?

My Confirmation Discoveries

Writing in a journal can help you focus your thoughts on the important things you have read and discussed with others on your confirmation journey. Sometimes, writing helps you clarify what you think and believe. What important things have you discovered about God, your church, and yourself on this journey? What questions about these ideas do you still have?

My Confirmation Relationships

The Bible speaks of Christians as being part of the same family, the church. Martin Luther thought highly of this church family and valued being a part of it. During your confirmation journey you have had a chance to learn from and with others in your church family. List their names, addresses, and phone numbers in the space provided so you can stay in touch after your confirmation journey ends.

Name	Relationship	Address	Phone Number

My Confirmation Responsibilities

Martin Luther discovered in the Bible that God's love exists prior to any of our good works. Jesus Christ died to forgive our sins and that act alone is sufficient to warrant our inclusion in God's kingdom. That puts new meaning in the word, *responsibility.* (Note the emphasis on the first part of the word.)

As forgiven sinners, we want to respond to God's love by imitating it in the way we live. What new *responsibilities* have occurred to you as you have studied what it means to be a follower of Jesus Christ? How will you respond?

My Confirmation Possibilities

God says in the First Commandment, "You shall have no other gods." While this may seem to restrict us, it actually gives us a great freedom. False gods derive their power from us. When we substitute other things, people, or activities as our gods, we must also assume the responsibility for keeping those gods in first place.

What new freedoms have you discovered during your confirmation journey? What ideas, relationships, and activities are you free to explore and pursue as a follower of Jesus? How does your family, church, and world respond to those freedoms?

My Confirmation Memories

From the beginning of God's special relationship with us, God has desired that we experience a special time as a regular part of our daily lives—a time devoted to studying God's Word and focusing on our relationship with God and from that, our relationship with other people.

What special times have you had on your confirmation journey? Who stands out in your memories of this journey? How will these special times affect your future?